Body Talk

The Straight Facts On Fitness, Nutrition & Feeling Great About Yourself!

Written by Ann Douglas and Julie Douglas

Illustrations by Claudia Dávila

MAPLE
TREE
PRESS

Maple Tree Press Inc.
51 Front Street East, Suite 200, Toronto, Ontario M5E 1B3
www.mapletreepress.com

Distributed in Canada by Raincoast Books
9050 Shaughnessy Street, Vancouver, British Columbia V6P 6E5

Distributed in the United States by Publishers Group West
1700 Fourth Street, Berkeley, California 94710

Dedication

To all the girls of the world who dare to be themselves.
– Ann and Julie

Cataloguing in Publication Data
Douglas, Ann, 1963-
    Body talk : the straight facts on fitness, nutrition & feeling great
about yourself! / written by Ann Douglas and Julie Douglas ;
illustrations by Claudia Dávila.

(Girl zone)
Includes index.
ISBN-13: 978-1-897066-62-1 (bound) / ISBN-10: 1-897066-62-7 (bound)
ISBN-13: 978-1-897066-61-4 (pbk.) / ISBN-10: 1-897066-61-9 (pbk.)

1. Girls—Health and hygiene—Juvenile literature. 2. Self-
perception—Juvenile literature. 3. Beauty, Personal—Juvenile
literature. 4. Body image—Juvenile literature. I. Dávila, Claudia
II. Douglas, Julie, 1988- III. Title. IV. Series.

RA777.25.D68 2006   j613'.04242   C2005-904765-8

Design & art direction: Claudia Dávila
Illustrations: Claudia Dávila
Photography: Rodrigo Moreno

We acknowledge the financial support of the Canada Council for the Arts, the Ontario
Arts Council, the Government of Canada through the Book Publishing Industry
Development Program (BPIDP), and the Government of Ontario through the Ontario
Media Development Corporation's Book Initiative for our publishing activities.

Printed in Belgium

C   D   E   F

CONTENTS

DARE TO BE YOU

Have you ever picked up a fashion magazine and wished that you looked more like the glamorous model or movie star on the cover? Or stared at yourself in the mirror, concentrating on all the things you would like to change about your appearance?

If you have, you've participated in a ritual so commonplace it just might show up as an Olympic event: the "sport" of beating yourself up about your appearance. Just imagine how the Olympic "competition" might look: a roomful of girls in front of full-length mirrors, waiting for the starter's pistol to be fired—or the blowdryer to be switched on—so that each can start listing her own flaws to outdo her opponents. Choruses of "I hate my hair," "my eyes are too small," "my nose is enormous," "my stomach's too big" would fill the room. Given the way girls can talk about themselves, we figure there'd be some pretty stiff competition for the gold medal!

But concerns about body image are no laughing matter. It's no joke when girls feel so pressured to conform to some crazy one-size-fits-all definition of beauty that they end up feeling bad about themselves and, in some cases, damaging their physical and emotional health. That's why we wrote this book: to remind you that you don't have to look like whatever supermodel happens to be the Flavor of the Month.

You can dare to be different.

You can dare to be you.

– Ann Douglas and Julie Douglas, age 14

Girl Talk In this book we quote some amazing girls who aren't afraid to "tell it like it is" about important issues. We hope that you enjoy meeting them as much as we did.

4

Chapter 1

BEAUTY: THEN & NOW

Did you know that blue hair was all the rage in ancient Egypt? Or that the ultimate sign of beauty in Mayan societies a thousand years ago was a corncob-shaped head? It's true. Mayan parents had to strap their baby's head to two boards so that the skull eventually assumed this highly unnatural elongated shape. What a price to pay for "beauty!"

As hard as it may be to believe, ideas about what makes a person beautiful change dramatically over time. What one generation considers beautiful, another generation may consider strange or even ugly. In fact, if your great-great-grandmother could step inside a time machine and meet today's generation of supermodels, she would probably find it hard to figure out how these bony and underweight young women could possibly be considered beautiful. That is, if she didn't faint dead away the moment she laid eyes on one of them strutting down the runway in a see-through blouse or microscopic miniskirt. After all, your great-great-grandmother grew up in an age when showing so much as your ankles in public was considered scandalous!

During the European Renaissance (in the 17th and 18th centuries), women used **lead-based powder** to whiten their complexions. It often led to muscle paralysis or even death. Other cosmetics were as deadly: eye shadows with lead and sulphide, and lip reddeners with mercuric sulfide.

Chew on This!

A hundred years ago, actress Lillian Russell, weighing 90 kg (200 lbs.), was considered a **great beauty**. Her flawless skin and plump figure made her more desirable than the also popular but skinny French actress Sarah Bernhardt.

Through Thick and Thin

Are you wondering how our attitudes about beauty and fashion have changed over the past two hundred years? Over the next few pages, we'll take you back in time to find out what types of bodies and fashions were popular at various points—and some of the shocking lengths women have been willing to go to in order to achieve "perfect beauty."

1800
Small, thin bodies are in, as is ghostly white skin. Tightly laced corsets achieve the smallest possible waists, but have major drawbacks: your stomach is so compressed you can hardly eat; your bladder is so squeezed you constantly run to the bathroom; and there's not enough room for your lungs to inflate! Some women even have ribs removed so they can lace their corsets tighter.

1830
A young minister named Sylvester Graham preaches against the evils of overeating. His diet of bland food is guaranteed to put your tastebuds to sleep. (Hard to believe the honey-flavored snack crackers bear his family name!)

1860s
Plump women with large bosoms and hips accentuated with a bustle are in vogue. A little extra weight is considered a sign of prosperity, and proof you are a nicer person. Thin women are considered mean and sour, while heavier women are thought to have a more pleasant nature and a better sense of humor.

1800

1863
The first bestselling diet book is published: *Letter on Corpulence* by William Banting. His diet calls for lean meat, dry toast, soft-boiled eggs, and a couple of alcoholic beverages each day!

1895
Artist Charles Dana Gibson's paintings of tall, athletic, self-confident "Gibson Girls" redefine the female ideal. Her measurements would be full-figured by today's standards: 96 cm (38 inch) bust, 69 cm (27 inch) waist, 114 cm (45 inch) hips.

1896
At his sanitarium, John Harvey Kellogg—brother of the corn-flakes guy—offers weight loss "treatments" with strange contraptions supposed to make the extra weight fall off.

1890s
Feathered hats are all the rage. In fact, they're so popular that some newspapers run articles warning about the impending extinction of certain types of birds due to the large number of feathers being used to decorate hats.

1898
Weight-loss fanatic Horace Fletcher promotes "the science of chewing"—if you chew each bite of food at least 20 times before swallowing, you'll get tired of chewing and repulsed by the food long before your stomach gets full. Fletcher is as fanatical about what comes out the other end. He weighs his stools and keeps a journal describing their color and texture.

1890s

1860s

1895

1907
The slim-figured showgirls in New York's Ziegfeld Follies kick off a trend toward thinness and dieting.

1921
The first beauty contest is held in America. Hotel owners in Atlantic City organize the event to get vacationers to stay beyond Labor Day.

1959
Barbie™ makes her debut. Her figure would be impossible for a real woman— 97 cm (39 inch) chest, 53 cm (21 inch) waist, 84 cm (33 inch) hips. In 40 years, enough Barbies™ would sell to circle the earth three-and-a-half times.

1920
The "Flapper" look is in style. Women bind their breasts to minimize their curves and achieve a slimmer, sportier, more boyish look. They wear shorter skirts, and cut and dye their hair. Now that dieting has become a national pastime, bathroom scales have made their way into most homes.

1953
There are five times as many diet articles published in women's magazines in 1953 than there were two years earlier.

1909
Department stores start placing cosmetics, such as face powder, lip salve, and rouge, in display cases instead of under the counter. Until then, cosmetics were considered nothing less than scandalous!

1930
The Flapper style gives way to a more full-figured look as we head into the Great Depression and World War II. Women have more serious concerns than the number on the bathroom scale.

1950s
The popularity of blonde movie star Marilyn Monroe leads three out of ten brunettes to dye their hair blonde. Womanly curves and flamboyant haircuts (e.g. the Beehive!) are definitely in.

1907

1920

1930

1950s

1966

1968
Feminists protest at the Miss America pageant in Atlantic City. They toss makeup, hair curlers, high heels, girdles, and bras into a waste receptacle that they dub "the freedom trash can."

1974
A black model appears on the cover of the fashion magazine *Vogue* for the very first time.

1990
The supermodel look comes into fashion. Instead of idealizing health and strength, this style is characterized by models with sickly, bone-thin bodies. While the average American woman is 163 cm (5 ft 4 inches) and 65 kg (144 lbs), the average model is 175 cm (5 ft 9 inches) and 56 kg (123 lbs).

1995
The U.S. Centers for Disease Control estimate 11 million women have eating disorders. (See page 36 for important information on eating disorders.)

1982
Actress Jane Fonda brings out the first in what will be a never-ending string of celebrity workout videos.

1966
The miniskirt arrives from Britain—a look made popular by an underweight 17-year-old British fashion model named Twiggy. She was 168 cm (5 ft 6 inches) and weighed just 40 kg (89 lbs).

1985
Inspired by singer and pop culture icon Madonna, many women start wearing their underwear as outerwear.

2000
Cosmetic surgery becomes increasingly popular with young women. The most popular procedures include liposuction (the suctioning of fat), rhinoplasty (a "nose job"), and breast implants (to make the breasts look larger).

1960   1965   1970   1975   1980   1985   1990   2000

1974

1982

1985

1990

Chapter 2

MIRROR, MIRROR

Many a horror movie is set in the House of Mirrors

at a carnival or amusement park. It's scary what strange tricks mirrors can play. They can convince you that you've suddenly become tall and skinny or short and fat, or distort your image in so many other weird and wonderful ways.

Many girls don't have to visit a house of mirrors to see a distorted image of themselves. When they look into the bathroom mirror, instead of seeing all the good things, they see only the things they don't like. And usually what they hate most is the shape or size of their bodies. You probably think your best friend looks great the way she is, and she probably thinks the same of you, but when it comes to ourselves, we can sometimes be so critical that we stop seeing straight.

Girl Talk

There's a lot of pressure for girls to look a certain way. They make fun of all the "ugly" kids for one thing. And if you don't wear a certain type of clothes, no one likes you.

– Jennifer

House of Mirrors or House of Horrors?

Girls who find it hard to look at themselves in the mirror have a negative body image, since they don't like their own bodies. Unfortunately, body-image problems are more common in girls than most people realize. Here are some facts that you may find both surprising and alarming:

One-third of girls ages 12 to 14 say that they would like to have cosmetic surgery to correct something they don't like about themselves.

More than **40 percent** of nine-year-old girls admit that they have tried dieting in an attempt to lose weight.

About **40 percent** of high-school girls of healthy weight and 49 percent of *underweight* high school girls say that they are trying to lose weight.

Your Own Worst Critic

Do you sometimes find yourself saying things

to yourself that you'd never say to your worst enemy? Here are some of the warning signs that you could be struggling with a negative body image:

You prefer to eat in **private** rather than in front of other people.

You spend a lot of time thinking about **food** and/or worrying about getting fat.

You constantly **compare** your body to other people's bodies (people in "real life" and people on TV or in magazines).

You say **mean things** about yourself when you're with other people.

You'd rather stay home **by yourself** than risk going to a party because you're afraid that other people will decide that you're unattractive and make fun of you.

You don't defend yourself when people make **jokes** about the way you look. (Or, even worse, you pretend to laugh along with them.)

You are **obsessed** with "improving" your appearance —dieting, begging your parents to let you have cosmetic surgery, or spending lots of money on clothes and cosmetics— because you feel ugly the way you are.

You feel **worse** about yourself after flipping through a magazine filled with photos of glamorous and abnormally thin models.

You hate **looking** at yourself in the mirror.

I think guys are more easily accepted and don't care as much about the way they look. They wear big clothes and throw on a cap and for them that looks "cool."

– Alicia

GirlTalk

Most role models are super beautiful and super skinny. It's not the same with boy role models.

– Laura

It's a Girl Thing
(Maybe, Maybe Not)

You might think that body-image problems are just "a girl thing." Think again. While girls feel pressured to transform themselves into beauty queens, boys feel pressured to look like bodybuilders. A recent study found that fully one-third of boys are unhappy with their bodies—unhappy enough, in fact, to feel the need to either lose weight or "bulk up" by building muscle. Even the action figures that young boys play with have become more muscular in recent years—so muscular that they no longer bear any resemblance to real human beings. If today's GI Joe™ action figure was 178 cm tall (5 ft 10 in), he'd have larger biceps than any bodybuilder in history. Bottom line? It's every bit as impossible for a boy to look like GI Joe™ as it is for a girl to look like Barbie™!

The Beautiful Truth

We all have bad hair days (and bad skin days!) but it's not healthy to be down on yourself every day. If you find that you feel bad about yourself more often than you feel good about yourself, you might want to take some concrete steps to turn your attitude around. You'll find some great ideas to help you do just that on the opposite page.

Chew on This!

A group of high school students in Ontario, Canada, recently staged a **fashion show** featuring student models of all shapes and sizes. The sole criterion for being selected as a model was being a physically active non-smoker. The event—Style in Motion: A Body Image Fashion Fair—won an award from Dietitians of Canada for helping to promote healthy lifestyles amongst teenagers.

Chew on This!

Body-image problems don't necessarily disappear once you become an adult. A 1997 study by *Psychology Today* magazine found that 56 percent of **adult women** are dissatisfied with their overall **appearance**, with 71 percent reporting that they don't like their stomachs, 66 percent indicating that they're unhappy with their weight, and 60 percent stating that they're unhappy with the size of their hips.

Let it Out...

Share your feelings

with someone you trust: a friend, a relative, a teacher. Choose someone who will really listen to you. But remember—what that person thinks about how you look isn't all that important. What matters is how *you* feel about *yourself*.

Start keeping **a journal**. If you find it difficult to tell other people how you're feeling, then write those feelings down. Not only will keeping a journal let you learn more about yourself and see how your thoughts and feelings change over time, it will also help you figure out some complicated feelings that are hard to put into words.

If you're not into writing, then think about using **art or music** to express how you feel. You can paint or draw a picture, write a song—whatever it takes to get your feelings out.

Make a list of the **ten things you like most** about your body—the color of your eyes, the curliness of your hair, the shape of your toes—and be sure to find ten!

Make a list of **ten terrific things** that your body allows you to enjoy: swimming, dancing, gymnastics, riding your bike, climbing a tree, and so on. The more you focus on your body's capabilities, the less hung up you'll be on its appearance.

The Top Ten...

Ask a friend

to make a list of ten things she likes or admires about you, and do the same thing for her. Then swap lists. You'll both end up feeling like a million bucks!

Start a new **family tradition**: at the dinner table, everyone says one thing they like or admire about each member of the family. Keep going around until you hit ten for each person.

Make Some Changes!

Set goals for

yourself that have nothing to do with how you look: maybe getting an "A" on a school project, passing your piano exam with flying colors, or improving your batting average in baseball.

Avoid reading magazines

or watching TV shows that make you feel bad about yourself. If you find an entertainment activity—going to see movies, watching music videos—causes your "ugly-o-meter" to start spinning around, it's time to switch to another activity.

When a negative thought pops into your head, imagine a giant red **stop sign** popping up right beside it.

Master the art of accepting **compliments**. It isn't conceited to be happy if someone says something nice about you. Compliments are supposed to make you feel good!

Chapter 3

THE ONE & ONLY YOU!

You probably already know that your body goes through a lot as you pass through puberty: your breasts develop, you get your menstrual period, and you experience other exciting bodily changes. Puberty happens at different times for different people (your body will know when it's ready). The way your body changes is also unique to you—as unique as the rest of the events in your life.

Chew on This!

During puberty, your skeletal mass (the weight of your skeleton), heart, lungs, liver, spleen, pancreas, glands, and sexual organs **double** in size. Believe it or not, even your eyes get larger—something that can have you running off to the optometrist's office complaining that you can no longer read the blackboard properly.

Me!

Me at 3 months!

My first steps

My 6th birthday

My grade 7 class photo

friends 4 ever

Me and Gloria

Chew on This!

Feel like you're the only person on the planet cursed with **acne**? Think again. Studies have shown that over 80 percent of people experience acne sometime in their lives.

Invasion of the Pimple Planters

What on Earth could have caused that outbreak of pimples that mysteriously showed up on your forehead and chin? It's not an invasion of alien "pimple planters" sent to do secret skin experiments on teenage girls while they sleep. The true culprit is something much less out-of-this-world: the hormonal changes of puberty.

The same hormones that trigger all the rest of the bodily changes that occur during puberty are also responsible for the skin changes that may be causing you grief. As your hormone levels rise, the sebaceous glands beneath your skin produce increasing quantities of sebum (oil that makes your skin soft and stretchy). If too much sebum is produced, the surface of your skin becomes very oily. Flakes of dead skin can get trapped in the sebum, leading to clogged skin pores, which ultimately result in eruptions of blackheads and whiteheads (a.k.a. "pimples" or "acne").

Chew on This!

Now that you've heard the bad news about skin problems, here's the **good news**: you can count your lucky stars that you were born female. Guys have much higher levels of the male sex hormone testosterone— a hormone that tends to send the sebaceous glands into overdrive— so guys tend to have a worse time with acne.

Skin smarts

While there's not much you can do to prevent pimples from occurring in the first place, there's plenty you can do to control them once they appear. (You'll note we said control them, not make them disappear altogether. Chances are you'll be battling pimples on and off for at least the next couple of years. It's part of the whole puberty turf.) In the meantime, here are a few tips on doing battle with pimples:

Practice good hygiene.
That means washing your face with pure, non-perfumed soap, drying it well, and not wearing makeup while you're dealing with an outbreak. (**Hint**: You can find pimple creams that double as concealers if you're self-conscious about that annoying pimple that decided to set up camp at the end of your nose.)

If you've got oily skin that is acne prone, be sure to slather on the **sunscreen** (ask your pharmacist to recommend a skin-friendly formulation) and limit the amount of time you spend in the sun. Rather than drying up your skin, prolonged sun exposure will trigger your skin's oil production—the last thing you need if acne is a problem for you.

Accept the fact that, no matter how carefully you take care of your skin, you'll probably experience an **outbreak** of pimples from time to time. They're most likely during the days leading up to your period (thanks to pre-menstrual hormonal changes) or if you're under a lot of stress (which can cause your hormone levels to go into over-drive, triggering an outbreak).

If over-the-counter acne products aren't doing the trick for you and/or you keep getting pimples that are large and painful or that leave scars, talk to your **family doctor** about the skin problems you're experiencing. Your doctor can tell if you require a prescription medication to control your acne.

Resist the temptation to squeeze or pick at your pimples. They'll disappear more quickly and be less likely to scar if you **leave them alone**.

Keep your **fingers** away from your face as much as possible. Even if they look clean, your fingers are loaded with dirt, oil, and bacteria that can aggravate your acne.

The Skinny on Skin

Your skin is the largest organ in your body. By the time you reach adult size, your skin will be about 1.8 square meters (19 square ft) in area and it will make up approximately one-sixth of your body weight.

Wondering what your skin's done for you lately? A lot! Your skin performs vital bodily functions, including temperature control—it helps regulate your body temperature by either cooling you down with sweat or making your body hair stand on end to help conserve heat. Your skin also protects your body from injury, infection, dehydration, and the sun's harmful UV rays. (You can give your skin help in the sun-protection department by putting on sunscreen before you hit the great outdoors.) These all sound like great reasons to take care of your skin.

Chew on This!

You're most likely to experience outbreaks of pimples on the parts of the body where your **sebaceous glands** are closest to the surface of the skin and located near hair follicles: on your face, your back, and your chest.

Girl Talk

Don't stress out over your skin. There is almost nothing you can do to change the fact that teenagers get pimples. It's a fact of life. Sure, wash your face every night with cleanser, but just remember: a zit or two is not a matter of life and death!

– Amanda

Hint: Masks are for your face—not your clothes, or the walls and furniture. Wear a T-shirt you can get dirty, and keep a towel handy to catch any "drips."

Spa Chez Vous

You don't have to head to a spa to be kind to your skin.
You can indulge in a lemon facial mask (for oily or normal skin)
or a cucumber facial mask (for dry skin) in your very own home.

Lemon mask
(oily or normal skin)

60 mL (1/4 cup) to 125 mL (1/2 cup)
of potter's clay (from craft supply store)

60 mL (1/4 cup) to 125 mL (1/2 cup)
of lemon juice concentrate

Place the ball of
clay in a bowl. Add the
lemon juice and roll the
clay around, absorbing the
juice. Apply the mask to your
face, being careful to avoid
your eyes. Leave on for 15 to
20 minutes. Rinse off with
warm water. Your face
should feel refreshed
and less oily.

Cucumber mask
(dry skin)

15 mL (1 tbsp.) plain yogurt
15 mL (1 tbsp.) cucumber (finely chopped)
15 mL (1 tbsp.) parsley (finely chopped)

Combine all
ingredients; mix until
smooth. Apply this creamy
mask to your face, being
careful to avoid getting it in
your eyes. For best results,
leave the mask on for 15 to
20 minutes. Then rinse off
with water. Your face will
be moisturized and
rejuvenated.

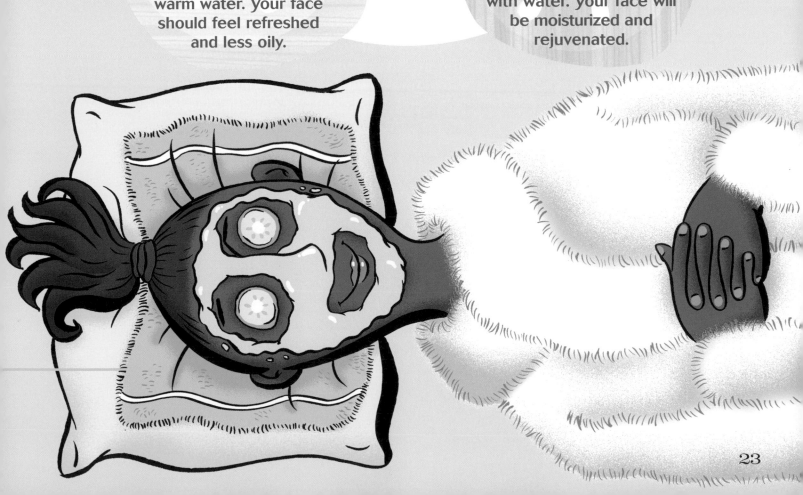

*The Facts on Fat

One of the huge changes that comes with puberty is growth, growth, growth. You can expect to gain approximately 20 percent of your adult height and 50 percent of your adult weight during this time.

When puberty hits, it changes the growth patterns of the previous few years. The rate of growth is more dramatic, like what you experienced when you were a baby. Some people even shoot up by a full 25 cm (10 in) by the time they're finished puberty—a process that can take as little as two years or as long as six years.

Of course, you don't just get taller: you also get heavier. Most girls gain between 18 and 23 kg (40 and 50 lbs) during puberty. This weight is deposited all over the body, with larger amounts of fat being deposited on the breasts and hips—the reason many girls start to develop classically female curves.

Does this added body fat mean that you're getting...well...fat? Not at all! You're simply leaving your "little girl" body behind and slipping into the body of a young woman. And because your body needs a certain amount of body fat on hand before you start menstruating, gaining additional body fat is an essential part of growing up.

You might go through a couple of months where you're gaining weight but not growing taller, or getting taller but not heavier. Part of the excitement is finding out just what kind of body you'll end up having. Just wait until your next growth spurt—Mother Nature isn't finished with you yet!

Chew on This!

While a **typical man** has approximately 15 percent body fat, a **typical woman** has 25 percent body fat.

Your Body is *Your* Body

You and your best friend are both the same height and the same weight, so you should be able to wear one another's jeans without any problem, right? Maybe, maybe not. If you both have the same basic body type—you're both muscular, for example—you might be able to have fun swapping clothes. But chances are you will each have a different percentage of body fat. This is because you came from different sets of parents, and their genes play a role in determining how fat or thin you end up being. This is not to say that you're "doomed" to be chubby if one or both of your parents are heavy. It just means that your odds of being heavy are a little bit higher than a tenth generation skinny person!

Being different isn't a bad thing. Just think how boring it would be if everyone had the same body type. It would be like walking down the cereal aisle at the grocery store and seeing nothing but corn flakes on the shelves—or channel surfing only to discover that every station was carrying the same show. So instead of wishing that you looked more like your best friend and less like yourself, celebrate the things that make you unique and special. Remember: you're the one and only you!

Chew on This!

Whose belly is this? That's what pop star **Nelly Furtado** had to ask herself when she caught a glimpse of a recent issue of the British men's magazine *FHM*. She was on the cover! Not only had Furtado not agreed to appear in the magazine, the photo that the magazine used had been digitally altered. She told a British radio interviewer: "There I am with a shirt that has actually been **digitally altered** to go to just below my chest, with a stomach that I don't recognize."

Girl Talk

My best friend thinks she's chubby and we have talked about it lots of times.

My advice to her was, yes, she is a little chubby, but we're friends and it doesn't matter how she looks.

It matters how she acts. She acts nice and is caring.

— Katelyn

What's Up, Doc?

Think you can tell if you have a weight problem by looking at the scale? Not exactly. The best way to find out whether you are carrying around extra weight or you're under a healthy weight for you is by talking to your doctor. She'll take into account such factors as your height, your age, your sex, your ethnic background, whether you're just starting or finishing puberty, and how physically active you tend to be, and then she'll suggest a weight range that is just right for you.

Girl Talk

"A girl should look like she wants to look."
– Eliza

Chew on This!

Studies have shown that black girls are less likely to be worried about their weight than white girls. One University of Arizona study found that most white girls wanted the same body type as supermodel Kate Moss— 170 cm (5 ft 7 inches) tall and 45 to 50 kg (100 to 110 lbs)—but that most black girls had **more realistic** attitudes about their bodies.

Chapter 4

DREAMS FOR SALE

The beauty, fashion, and weight-loss industries are in the business of selling dreams. They try to convince people that wearing the right lipstick, buying an outfit in this season's hottest color and style, or losing weight is a "one size fits all" solution to whatever problems they might be facing in life. Not getting along with your parents? Just broke up with your boyfriend? Worried that you won't be chosen for the soccer team or do well on your math test? Improving your appearance will solve all your problems—or so these companies would have you believe.

These companies are, after all, in the business of making money—the more you spend, the better their profits will be. And so we have a never-ending parade of new beauty products and changes in clothing colors and styles from season to season.

Sometimes the techniques marketers use can be downright deceiving. Unwary consumers can find themselves being conned by the manufacturer of some "miracle product" that promises to help you "get rid of unwanted body hair forever" or "eliminate wrinkles before they start." Maybe you should wonder if the editor of a beauty magazine is more interested in pushing its advertisers' products than in providing its readers with unbiased information about those products, or if a food manufacturer's line of "light" or "low-fat" snack foods are anything but low in calories. The best way to fight back against Corporate America is to arm yourself with the facts—the very thing we'll be helping you to do over the next few pages.

Lip Service

Why hit the drugstore to load up on beauty stuff when you can make your own? Here's a recipe for homemade lip balm that smells and tastes great and that will leave your lips feeling soft and smooth.

Luscious Lip Balm

15 mL (1 tbsp.) of refined beeswax beads
125 mL (1/2 cup) of sweet almond oil
10 mL (2 teaspoons) of lemon or tangerine essential oil

Place the almond oil in a glass measuring cup. Add beeswax beads and melt on low heat in the microwave (you might have to take it out, stir, and return to heat some more).

Stir with a spoon and allow to cool slightly before adding essential oil. Pour into small glass or plastic jars with tight-fitting lids.

Chew on This!

The cosmetics industry rings up around **$45 billion** U.S. in sales each year, with 30 percent of all sales being made in North America. In fact, each second, 25 tubes of lipstick are sold in the United States alone.

Hint: You can find beeswax beads and the oils you need in a health-food or craft supply store.

Operation Brainwash

By the time you start high school you will be exposed to 350,000 television and print advertisements, over 50 percent of which stress being beautiful and thin. Talk about being brainwashed! To make matters worse, many of the images have been altered—if even supermodels need to have their pictures "fixed" to take out pimples and wrinkles, there's something wrong with our beauty standards, don't you think?

Of course, it can be fun to paint your nails, color your hair, and play around with your appearance. Unfortunately, many of the ads about these beauty products lose sight of the fact that using these products is supposed to be a fun way of expressing yourself— not something you have to do in order to measure up to someone else's beauty idea.

Chew on This!

Women's magazines are known for sandwiching articles on **dieting** between recipes for chocolate cake, or placing an article on eating disorders across from an ad designed to play on **insecurities** you may have about your body.

Chew on This!

A recent study showed **69** percent of girls base their ideal body image on pictures they see in magazines, and **47** percent say that looking at these images makes them want to lose weight.

Here are some things **YOU** can do to fight back against Operation Brainwash:

Look at the different ways that girls and women are **depicted in ads** in magazines. In what ways do the "ideal" girls and women in these ads compare to photos of the "real" girls and women you know?

If you come across an ad that really offends you, **write a letter** to the company that produced the ad and send a copy of your letter to the magazine or newspaper that printed the ad or the television station that aired it.

If you find an ad that makes you feel good, consider writing to that manufacturer, too. Better yet, ask your health teacher if you can set up a **Hall of Fame** wall in your classroom to spotlight all the positive ads you find in newspapers and magazines.

Next time you're standing in line at the store looking at the magazines, be choosy. Don't automatically spend your money on the one featuring an article on weight loss or on making yourself look more beautiful. Don't give in to **our culture's fixation** with weight and beauty.

Make a list of all the **women you admire**. These could be people you know in real life or women you've read about in newspapers or seen on TV. Think about why you admire them. Is it their looks, their achievements, or their personalities that you find so inspiring?

Help spread the word about **positive body image**. Get your friends talking about what they're seeing in the media. Make sure they realize that they don't have to take all those advertising messages at face value.

Listen carefully to the types of words **television advertisers** use to convince you to buy their products. Is their goal to make you feel worse about yourself, or to convince you that their products will make you feel better about yourself? Or both?

Playing with Knives

There was an explosion of interest in cosmetic surgery during the 1990s, according to the American Society of Plastic Surgeons. By the year 2000, nearly twice as many North Americans underwent cosmetic surgery as did eight years earlier. And, what's more, a growing number of these patients were young women.

Chew on This!

Most doctors are reluctant to perform cosmetic surgery on young people whose bodies haven't finished developing, but others are happy to have their business. In 1998, more than **22,000 American teenagers** had cosmetic surgery procedures that cost thousands of dollars each.

Chew on This!

Some people are so desperate to lose weight that they have their **stomachs stapled**. This weight-loss surgery can have very unpleasant side effects, including nausea, weakness, and diarrhea after eating. There's also the risk of more serious complications, including abdominal hernias, gallstones, and nutritional deficiencies. Some people have died from complications—the ultimate price to pay for a shot at thinness that might be temporary!

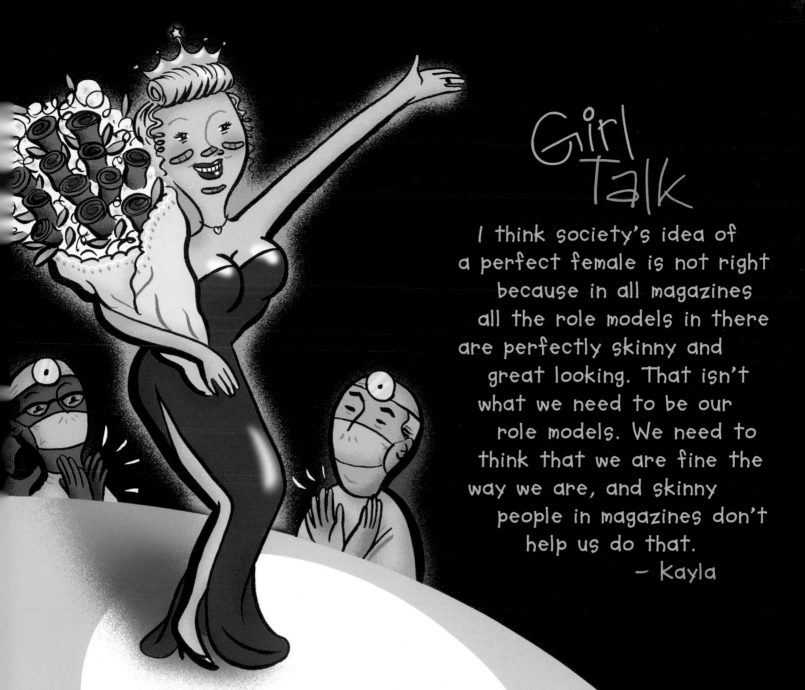

Here She Is...Miss Cosmetic Surgery!

You have to wonder what Juliana Borges was thinking as she was crowned Miss Brazil 2001: how excited she was to be realizing her life-long dream of winning the beauty pageant, or of the 23 cosmetic surgeries she went through to walk away with the title.

To increase her chances of winning the pageant, Juliana had subjected herself to cosmetic surgery on her cheeks, jaw, chin, nose, ears, and breasts. She had also arranged to have her birthmarks removed and to have fat deposits vacuumed away through a surgical procedure known as liposuction.

Juliana wasn't the only contestant in the Miss Brazil pageant to spend a lot of time at a surgeon's office. It was later discovered that one-third of the 27 finalists had had one or more cosmetic surgeries! One of the pageant organizers noted in the aftermath of the scandal, "It's a war out there." Unfortunately, what the organizer failed to note is that the casualties in this particular war were the contestants! Cosmetic surgery isn't just expensive: it can sometimes be painful and risky as well.

Fat Profits

We've all seen the dramatic "before and after" photos in weight-loss ads: shots of gorgeous, smiling women who have supposedly lost large amounts of weight while following a particular diet or using a particular product. The message always seems the same: "I was miserable while I was fat, but now that I've lost weight, my life is perfect!" But, as with all advertisements, you have to read between the lines or at least look carefully at the fine print.

The weight-loss industry in North America rings up about $55 billion U.S. in sales each year. Unfortunately, many of those dollars are spent on products that are highly ineffective. The best way to protect yourself against weight-loss scams is to learn to read the fine print in weight-loss advertisements. On the opposite page is a fake, but typical, weight-loss ad along with the types of questions that should run through your head when you read an ad like this. It is similar to ads you can find in many magazines and on TV.

Chew on This!

In recent years, the U.S. Food and Drug Administration (FDA) has banned 111 ingredients found in over-the-counter diet products because they were proven to be ineffective or downright **dangerous**.

Chew on This!

Next time you see a TV commercial for a weight-loss program or diet product, watch for the **fine print** on the screen. Chances are you'll discover that the results depicted in the commercial are "not typical." ("Typical" results would be someone not losing any weight at all or—even worse—actually gaining weight!)

How much weight can you reasonably expect to lose when you're sleeping? This sounds kind of fishy!

How many patients were involved in the study? Were the studies performed on people or animals? If the laboratory was so prestigious, why don't they give you its name?

Enjoy guaranteed weight loss while you sleep!

If this method of losing weight is truly effortless, why do people waste their time exercising or watching what they eat? Remember: if it sounds too good to be true, it probably is!

Thanks to a miraculous discovery by a team of doctors at a very prestigious research laboratory, you can now lose weight effortlessly while you sleep. There's no need to exercise or watch your diet: the pounds will just melt away. Preliminary findings indicate that the product is safe, natural, and highly effective. Finally the secret to permanent weight loss can be yours, thanks to this amazing breakthrough.

If it is that amazing, it wouldn't be a secret. It would be on the front page of every newspaper!

Do you really want to take a product that is unproven? Preliminary means that the jury is still out. No one knows for sure that the product is "safe, natural, and highly effective"—at least not yet.

Chapter 5

WHAT'S EATING YOU?

When some girls say that they're "dying to be thin," they aren't exaggerating. Their desire to lose weight is so strong that they may be putting their very lives at risk. These girls have what is known as an eating disorder (boys can also have eating disorders, but these conditions are less common in boys). One in ten girls with an eating disorder dies and many are left with permanent damage to their bodies.

There are three basic types of eating disorders:

Anorexia

a condition in which a girl with an intense fear of gaining weight starves herself and/or exercises excessively to keep her body weight abnormally low. Anorexia can cause damage to the heart or the liver, and can lead to osteoporosis (fragile bones).

Bulimia

a condition in which a girl eats a large quantity of food, then gets rid of it by vomiting, taking drugs, or exercising excessively. Bulimia can lead to osteoporosis or heart problems. Repeated vomiting can damage the throat and teeth; using laxatives can hurt the intestines.

Binge Eating Disorder

a condition in which a girl eats a large quantity of food in a short period of time (it is like bulimia, but without getting rid of the food eaten). After they binge, these girls feel out of control, depressed, or guilty. Binge eating can cause significant weight gain.

Anorexia takes on a life of its own.... You don't look at yourself properly. It consumes you. It is you. It affects your health, your personality, and your brain chemistry. – recovering anorexic Heather Thompson, 26, in an article at MayoClinic.com

Girl Talk

Identifying an Eating Disorder

How to help a friend who has an eating disorder

If you suspect that your friend has an eating disorder, you may be scared and upset and unsure of what to do. Here are a few tips:

Let your friend know

that you care and are worried about her eating habits: "I'm worried about you because you never eat lunch anymore." "I think you've lost a lot of weight. I'm really scared for you." "You always run to the bathroom right after lunch, and when you come back, you smell like you've just thrown up. I'm really concerned about you."

Encourage

your friend to do things she enjoys, like playing with you and your dog or coming to a sleepover. It's important for her to focus on things other than her weight and relationship with food.

Let your friend know that you want to help.

Encourage her to talk to your school nurse or another adult who can help her. If she's not willing to do this, try to line up some help for her. It's not being a tattle-tale: you're being a caring and concerned friend.

Remind your friend

how special she is to you and try to help her to see her own strengths. Rather than focussing on how she looks (she's already too obsessed with her appearance as it is) focus on the things that you admire most about her: her Web-design skills, her singing voice, or the way she tells jokes.

Listen

to what your friend has to say. Don't be surprised if she denies having an eating disorder or gets angry with you for suggesting it. She may feel afraid, ashamed, and guilty about the situation.

Note:

If you think you may have an eating disorder yourself, be your own best friend. Seek out the help you need and deserve. Don't let an eating disorder destroy your life.

She comes home to an empty house after school and **eats everything** in sight.

She eats only a **small amount** of the food on her plate. She may just move it around, or wrap it up and throw it away when no one is looking.

She is **obsessed** with keeping her weight low to model, act, or play sports where thin bodies are highly valued.

She starts spending a huge amount of time **exercising** and gets quite upset if someone suggests that she might be "overdoing it."

Do **YOU** or someone you know have an eating disorder?

Here are some of the warning signs that might indicate someone who has a problem with food.

She starts wearing **baggy clothes** to hide how thin she is, and to cover the fine layer of hair growing all over her body (as it tries to keep itself warm.)

She is **irritable**, moody, and having difficulty concentrating at school.

She feels **nausea**, headaches, or fatigue. Her periods have stopped (or they never started) and she may be smoking, drinking, and/or using marijuana.

She goes on a **strict diet** after being teased about her weight, starts making herself vomit or taking laxatives or diuretics to try to control her weight.

She **skips breakfast and lunch**, gets out of eating dinner, and goes on a binge in the evening or the middle of the night when there's no one watching what she's eating.

She **refuses to eat** meat, eggs, milk—foods she mistakenly assumes will make her fat—and is so weak she can't perform at a dance, gymnastics, or cheerleading event.

She **complains** repeatedly about the size or shape of her body.

She **starves herself** before a sporting event in order to drop a few pounds, and then eats nonstop for a day or two after the event.

She starts spending more time **alone**. She simply doesn't have the energy to do things anymore.

Why Dieting Doesn't Work

What the weight-loss industry will never tell you, of course, is that fad diets can actually make you put on weight. Dieting scrambles the signals that tell your body when it's had enough, so you keep eating after your stomach's full. You can also go into fat-preservation mode: your body burns food more slowly so that its food supply will last longer—something that was helpful in times of famine, but not today when there's a fast-food restaurant on every corner!

Your body's desire to hold on to its fat stores makes it difficult to lose weight, and also makes it easy to quickly regain any weight you managed to lose following the latest (but not necessarily greatest) fad diet. This is because you have messed with your metabolism, the "computer" that controls the speed at which your body burns food. When you go back to eating normally, your body gains weight because you've trained it to survive on less food.

But that's not all the bad news when it comes to dieting. While you're losing weight, you lose water, fat, and muscle tissue. And any weight you gain back after going off a diet is made of up fat rather than muscle. So you usually end up having a greater proportion of fat tissue than you did before you started trying to lose weight. And because fat tissue burns fewer calories than muscle tissue, you may continue to gain weight long after you go off the diet.

So what gives you the greatest chances of success staying at a healthy weight through your life? Staying active and eating a well-balanced diet. Check out the next two chapters!

Girl Talk

Nobody is perfect, so don't try to be. It will only cost you in the future. Your life is not worth the risk of being thin. — Nancy

Chew on This!

Girls who diet more than once a week are 4 times more likely than other girls to **smoke**. Researchers at Boston Children's Hospital think the reason is that dieting creates nicotine cravings. The long list of smoking-related health risks should make anyone think twice about that!

International No Diet Day

is May 5. Founded in the United Kingdom, people give up dieting for a day and consider if dieting has improved their overall health and happiness. (Mostly, the answer is no.). Celebrations include tossing bathroom scales in the trash or talking about really bad fad diets from the past.

Chew on This!

You tried to convince your best friend not to go on a crash diet, but she did it anyway. She's just phoned you to tell you that she's lost 2 kg (5 lbs) in five days. You don't have the heart to tell her that most of what she's lost is water, not fat. When your body starts drawing on its stores of carbohydrates—the energy it packed away in your cells for just such a moment of "famine"—a large amount of **water** is flushed from your body. Each 1/2 kg (1 lb) of carbohydrates in your body is stored with 1 to 2 kg (3 to 4 lbs) of water. If you use 1/2 kg (1 lb) of carbohydrate stores, you automatically drop 1 to 2 kg (3 to 4 lbs) in water weight, too. The moment you start eating normally again, however, that weight comes right back on as the new carbohydrate stores start packing away their own supply of water.

41

Hungering for More

Sometimes people eat for reasons other than hunger. They eat because they're upset about something and they mistakenly think that eating food will make them feel better, because they are bored, or simply because the food is there.

Because it's there

Eating food because it's there is a trap you'll want to avoid. (Some people who fall into this trap say that they're on the "see food" diet: they see food and they eat it!) Rather than eating that bag of potato chips simply because you know that it's there in the kitchen cupboard, why not hold off until you're actually hungry? You'll enjoy them a whole lot more if your body is ready for food.

Emotional eating

Eating for comfort when you are upset ("emotional eating") is an unhealthy way of dealing with life's ups and downs. Do you think that eating that bag of cookies is going to somehow make you feel better? Unfortunately, emotional eating only adds to your problems. Not only does it fail to solve the problem that led you to reach for food in the first place, it could also lead to more weight than is healthy, or even an eating disorder. A smarter way to deal with the underlying problem is to find ways to deal with it head on: face up to your feelings of anger or disappointment, or brainstorm possible solutions. You might also find it helpful to start keeping a "food journal" so that you can start to make links between your emotions and your eating habits. Or learn how to use relaxation breathing, yoga, or other stress-management techniques for coping with whatever curveballs life is tossing your way.

Girl Talk

Sometimes we need to let our brains and our bodies take a rest. I like to relax by reading a good book, watching my favorite TV show, or just looking out the window and daydreaming sometimes. I also enjoy playing board games with my family. I find it very relaxing after a busy week.

– Leah

Eating because you're bored

Eating out of boredom is a habit that can get you into trouble. If you open the refrigerator and grab a snack each time you're feeling at loose ends, you end up giving your body food it doesn't actually need. A better solution: find non-food ways of entertaining yourself if you find yourself feeling restless. Bounce a basketball around, pick up the phone and call a friend, or dive into a brand new book—whatever it takes to avoid hitting the refrigerator simply because you've got nothing better to do.

Chew on This!

"I'll have a side order of classical music with my burger." A study at Johns Hopkins University found that people who listen to **rock music** while they are eating eat more rapidly, shovel in more food, and are more likely to ask for second helpings than people who listen to more soothing types of music.

Chapter 6

LET'S GET PHYSICAL

You've heard it before: one of the most important—and definitely the most fun— parts of looking and feeling great in your body is being active.

A hundred years ago, people didn't have to hit the gym to stay strong and healthy. They got plenty of physical activity walking to school or work, doing chores at home, or working at physically demanding jobs like farming. The average person today burns between 300 and 400 fewer calories a day compared with fifty years ago.

Today, we live in a highly automated society where labor-saving devices—from dishwashers to escalators to cars—make it increasingly difficult for us to get the physical activity our bodies need to stay healthy. We don't even have to get off the couch to change the TV channel or turn up the volume on the CD player: remote controls take care of that with the push of a button.

Chew on This!

If you can't fit in big chunks of exercise, work in little ones instead. A recent study at the University of Pittsburgh revealed that **short bouts** of exercise sprinkled throughout the day are every bit as effective as long ones performed all at once.

Some kids are couch potatoes. TV can be addictive thanks to those cliffhanger episodes. Video games can be addictive too: you keep wanting to get better and better or to get farther in the game. — Amanda

45

The Three Big Myths

Growing numbers of North Americans are joining the ranks of the couch potato. According to the National Center for Health Statistics, just 40 percent of American adults exercise as often as they should; and 25 percent are completely inactive. It's never too young to start to fight against a future like that! Despite what's at stake—our very health and well-being—there's a lot of misinformation out there about physical fitness. How many of these fitness-related myths below have you heard?

The Three Biggest Myths About Exercise

Myth: Exercise is boring.

Fact: Being physically active is anything but boring—unless you consider skateboarding, rollerblading, cross-country skiing, and dancing to music with a friend nothing but a big yawn. Exercise can be walking, riding a bike, tossing around a Frisbee, swimming, skating, or a million other things. The key to making it fun is to find an activity you enjoy and, better yet, a friend to enjoy it with.

Myth: Exercising takes too much time.

Fact: Actually, you can enjoy the benefits of physical fitness by being active for just 20 minutes at a time, three times each week. Squeeze in a mini-workout at least every other day. The secret to getting physically fit is to find ways to make exercise fit in your regular routine. It'll soon become as automatic as brushing your teeth.

Myth: Exercise leaves you tired and sore.

Fact: If this is how you feel after being physically active, you're pushing your body to do things it's not yet ready to do. Not to say you won't ever be able to run 5 km (3 miles), but you might have to start out walking it! The good news is that regular exercise does exactly the opposite—it leaves you feeling energized and strong.

Soothing Soak

Reward yourself! You overdid it a bit in the exercise department, and your muscles are calling for a **time-out**. Why not head for the nearest bathtub and treat yourself to this soothing soak? Simply pour a little bit of eucalyptus essential oil (available at craft stores and health-food stores) into your bath. It will help to relieve your aches and pains.

Girl Talk

My favorite way to relax and unwind is to watch a TV show or a movie. Other ways I like to relax are by taking a bath, or going into my room and listening to music. — Kayla

Gym Klutz

Contrary to popular belief, you don't have to be a natural-born athlete to be physically fit. Even if gym class was never your favorite subject, you can still find ways to make exercise a fun and enjoyable part of your life.

In the summer, I get more exercise, but in the winter, I don't want to go outside. I have gym class twice a week, but do you really call getting hit in the head with a badminton racket exercise?!! – Jennifer

Girl Talk

My gym teacher does a really good job of making gym class fun and interesting. He lets us go on the trampoline and has taken us cross-country and downhill skiing. – Alicia

Exercise makes you **stronger.** It helps you build muscle tissue. And since muscle tissue is firmer and more attractive than fat tissue, being physically fit improves your appearance.

Exercise is good for your **skin.** After a workout, the blood rushes through your skin, something that helps to wash away waste, leaving you with a healthy glow.

Exercise jumpstarts your **metabolism.** Your body burns more calories during and after you exercise.

Exercise makes your **heart** strong. It lessens your chances of developing heart disease down the road (one of the leading killers of North Americans) and also improves your stamina so you can play longer and harder without huffing and puffing, today!

Still not sold on exercise? Here are some bonuses!

Exercise helps to **relax** you and improve your mood. One study found that a person's anxiety levels drop for more than two hours after a workout—a terrific reason to hit the pavement running (or walking!).

Exercise is the perfect **social** activity. You're bound to make new friends if you sign up for a dance class, start going to the gym, join a team, or ride your bike with a friend or group a few evenings a week.

Exercising with a **friend** allows you to sneak in a visit while you're doing something healthy for your body. (The alternative—talking on the phone while you raid the refrigerator—isn't nearly so body-friendly!)

Exercising alone allows you to take **time for yourself.** Whether you use this time to day-dream, write songs in your head, brainstorm solutions to problems troubling you, or simply enjoy a much-needed break from your pesky brother, it's time for you.

Exercise makes you more **alert** and more creative—good news if you're about to study for a test or write a composition for English class.

Exercise gives you an **energy burst** that lasts long after you finish working out. It also helps ensure you'll get a good night's sleep so that you'll wake up feeling refreshed and ready to tackle whatever adventures happen to come your way.

Exercise keeps you **healthy.** It gives your immune system a bit of a boost so that you're less likely to pick up every cold and flu bug that's going around.

Staying On Track

Here are some tips on getting active and staying motivated.

Stop viewing exercise as a form of torture. Instead of thinking of it as something you have to do, think of it as something **you want** to do. That means finding an activity that you will genuinely enjoy.

Take **small steps** to get more activity into your life. Instead of getting a drive to the mall, ride your bike, in-line skate, or walk there instead. Get in the habit of doing this and soon your energy level will increase.

Find an **exercise buddy.** You'll have such fun, working out will be like play! Choose someone who enjoys the same activities you do, and at the same pace. It's not as much fun to be left in the dust by a total jock, or to always be waiting for someone to catch up to you.

Set realistic **goals.** Don't plan an exercise schedule that would have an Olympic athlete begging for mercy. If your goals are too high, you're likely to get discouraged and might end up not exercising at all.

Levels of physical fitness are plummeting for people of all ages, so why not try to find ways to get fit **as a family?** (Hint: If you're not too keen about being seen working out with Mom and Dad at the gym, suggest a hike in the woods instead.)

Chew on This!

Only **25** percent of sixth-grade girls and **29** percent of eighth-grade girls report that they exercise four or more times each week outside of school.

Chew on This!

In the late 19th century, women were **discouraged** from exercising, as it was thought to cause mental or reproductive problems. Studying was also supposed to be harmful to women because it diverted blood to the brain and away from other organs. Clearly, it wasn't the women who had the brain problems!

Figure out how you're going to fit activity into your life. Don't leave things to chance, as it's too easy to fall back into old (inactive) habits. You'll dramatically increase your odds of sticking with it if you **schedule** your workouts in advance.

Variety is the spice of life. If you go bike riding today, find a different activity for tomorrow. If you're bored with exercising in your basement, hit the great outdoors.

Think about what you're **eating,** particularly on days when you're exercising. Giving your body the right fuel provides the energy boost you need to make workouts invigorating and enjoyable, not draining.

Exercising to **music** is fun. Grab your boom box or watch music videos—just put a song in your heart and a bounce in your step.

Next time a friend suggests watching TV or playing video games, suggest an active **alternative** instead: a trip to the park, bowling a few frames, an afternoon of ice or in-line skating, or a pick-up game on the basketball courts.

Try a **new** fitness activity every couple of months. Check out the library video rack—skateboarding tricks or Latin dance moves are just a spin away!

Give yourself a **break!** Listen to your body—if you feel tired or unmotivated take a guilt-free day off. And return with renewed energy the next.

Chapter 7

FOOD FOR THOUGHT

Chew on This!

Have you heard people describe things like chocolate bars and potato chips as "bad" foods and apples and carrots as "good" foods? While a lot of people tend to classify foods this way, there's actually room in a healthy diet for even the most sugary and high-fat foods—just **not every day**. Some nutritionists prefer to classify foods as **everyday** and **sometimes** foods rather than "good" and "bad" ones.

If you've heard music performed live, you already know what makes such a performance so exciting: the music the various instruments make when they play together is far more impressive than the music that any individual instrument can make on its own.

The same thing applies to eating: the greater the variety of foods in your diet, the better off you'll be from a nutritional standpoint. No single food can deliver all the nutrients our bodies need. As delicious and nutritious as the individual foods in your diet may be, you end up with a more interesting diet and a healthier body if you get in the habit of eating a variety of different foods. Choose foods from each of the four basic food groups and ensure that you don't get into a nutritional rut: eating the same foods for breakfast (yawn), lunch (yawn), and dinner (big yawn) day after day.

And while we're talking nutrients, here's another important point: don't make the mistake of thinking that taking a vitamin pill every morning will get you off the hook when it comes to eating properly. There are compounds in foods that you can't get from a vitamin pill. And, what's more, vitamins compete with one another when it's time to be absorbed into the body. If you take all your vitamins at one time, not all of the vitamins will be fully absorbed by your body—the more aggressive vitamins will win out! On the other hand, if you get your vitamins by eating a variety of different foods over the course of a day, the more timid vitamins can sneak into your body while the aggressive ones aren't paying attention.

Finding the Balance

When you're deciding what to eat for a balanced diet, make sure you choose foods from each of the four main food groups: grains, vegetables and fruits, milk products, and meats and alternatives. For variety and healthy choices, think about making the food on your plate a colorful medly.

Grain products

Aim to eat **6–11 servings** from this group each day (1 serving = 1 slice of bread; 1/2 bagel; or 125 mL (1/2 cup) of cooked rice or pasta).

Grain products are what put the "go" in your "get-up-and-go," rich in the carbohydrates that give your body an instant energy burst. They are also an excellent source of vitamins and nutrients as well as dietary fiber, to fill you up and help keep your bowels moving. Nutritionists suggest that you work some whole-grain and enriched grain products into your diet on a regular basis.

Vegetables and fruits are rich in vitamins as well as disease-fighting compounds called phytochemicals. They're also a terrific source of dietary fiber. Choose dark green and orange fruits and vegetables like broccoli, spinach, carrots, squash, cantaloupe, oranges—some of the most nutrient-rich foods around.

Vegetables and fruits

Aim to eat **5–9 servings** of vegetables and fruits each day (1 serving = a medium-sized apple, potato, or orange; 125 mL (1/2 cup) of fruit juice or chopped vegetables; 250 mL (1 cup) of raw leafy vegetables; or 180 mL (3/4 cup) of vegetable juice).

Milk products

Aim to eat **2–3 servings** of milk products each day (1 serving = 250 mL (1 cup) of milk or yogurt; or 40 to 55 grams (1 1/2 to 2 ounces) of cheese).

Calcium is one of those jack-of-all-trades minerals. And milk products provide your body with the calcium that it needs to regulate your blood pressure, help your muscles contract, assist your blood in clotting, and—as you probably know—keep your bones healthy and strong. That's why it's important to include foods like cheese, yogurt, and/or milk in your diet on a daily basis.

Meat and alternatives provide your body with protein to build bones, organs, tendons, muscle, cartilage, hair, nails, teeth, and skin. Protein is responsible for bodily functions that include fighting disease and transporting oxygen throughout the body.

Meat and alternatives

Aim to eat **2–3 servings** from this group each day (1 serving = 55 to 85 grams (2 to 3 ounces) of cooked meat; 1 egg; 125 mL (1/2 cup) of dry beans, cooked; 30 mL (2 tbsp.) peanut butter; or 100 grams (3 1/2 ounces) of tofu).

Chew on This!

Next time you're sitting in class, look at the kids sitting on either side of you. Odds are one of the three of you isn't eating well enough to get the **nutrients** his or her body needs. (Let's hope it isn't you!) Research shows that one-third of teenagers fail to obtain the recommended daily allowances for vitamins A, B6, C, and E, as well as calcium, iron, folic acid, and zinc.

Chew on This!

Only 77 percent of sixth-grade and 69 percent of eighth-grade girls report that they eat **vegetables** daily.

The Rest of the Story

As you've no doubt noticed, not every food neatly fits into one of the four food groups listed here. These foods fall into the "other foods" category—including such foods as spreads, oils, jams, honey, snack foods, soda pop, coffee, tea, water, and condiments. While some of these foods are low in nutrients—you won't build a lot of muscle downing glass after glass of cola, for example—other foods, like water, play an important role in a healthy diet. In fact, nutritionists recommend that you drink six to eight glasses of water each day in order to keep your body well hydrated.

There's also room in your diet for some high-fat foods—particularly if you're going through a growth spurt or you play sports on a regular basis. But it's a good idea to start developing a taste for some low-fat foods at the same time, so that you can start choosing lower fat foods more often as you get older and your rapid growth spurts become a thing of the past.

Reading the Signals

The best way to eat

is the one that comes naturally: paying attention to your body's hunger and fullness "signals." Your body is equipped to tell you when it's time to eat—your stomach feels slightly empty and you start thinking about food. Your body can also tell you when it's time to put on the brakes. If you start feeling full in the middle of dinner, your body is letting you know it's time to give your fork a rest.

If you ignore your body's hunger signals, it will try even harder to get your attention. You'll start feeling lightheaded, you'll have difficulty concentrating on anything but food, and you'll develop a killer headache. When you finally give in to your hunger pangs, chances are you'll go overboard, stuffing your face with any food that isn't nailed down.

If you ignore your body's fullness signals, you'll also experience some physical discomfort. Your stomach will start feeling overly full, you may start to feel sick, and you'll be more inclined to flop out on the couch than to hop on your bike or skateboard.

Check out the handy Hunger Scale on the opposite page and get more in touch with your body's signals. Don't be surprised if your food intake varies a bit from day to day: you'll likely have days when you are positively ravenous and other days when you couldn't care less about food. What matters is that you let your body's appetite guide you instead of going by anybody else's ideas about how much you should—or shouldn't—be eating.

Hunger Scale
How You're Feeling

Stuffed — +5

You've made too many trips to the all-you-can-eat buffet. You feel so tired and stuffed you'd like nothing more than to take a nap. Groan!

+4 — **The Bulging Stomach**

You've eaten so much food your stomach feels uncomfortably full. It might even hurt. You're already wishing you passed up that third piece of cake.

The Bloated Feeling — +3

You feel bloated and uncomfortable. Suddenly, your jeans feel too tight. Could they have shrunk in the dryer?

+2 — **More Than Satisfied**

Your stomach is saying, "No," but your mind is telling you "Yes" to a few more bites, even though you're no longer really tasting your food.

Just A Bit Over — +1

You may have overindulged a bit, but you stopped before you got too uncomfortable. You may even have managed to leave something on your plate.

✓ — **Satisfied**

You're content, happy, and energized. You're neither stuffed nor starving, so you're able to focus on things other than food. Right on!

Mild Hunger — -1

It's been three or four hours since you last ate. You've got a mild hollow feeling in your stomach and you're starting to think about food. Where did you leave that granola bar?

-2 — **Thinking About Food**

You're hungry enough to fantasize about food. Hope your teacher isn't giving hints about the big test coming up, because you're not really paying attention!

Empty — -3

Your urge to eat is so strong you can't think of anything but filling the hollow pit in your stomach. It's almost impossible to concentrate on anything around you.

-4 — **Famished**

Your stomach is rumbling and you've become irritable and cranky. Anyone who gets between you and the vending machine is in trouble! You're starting to feel weak and nauseous.

Too Far Gone — -5

You have a headache, you feel dizzy, and you've lost your coordination. You've gone so long without food that you're too tired to eat. All you want to do is go to sleep.

Smart Start

The word "breakfast" means to break (end) the fast (the period of not eating) that occurred while you were sleeping. Breakfast is your chance to fuel up your body with the energy it needs to get through the day. Unfortunately, many girls choose to start their day running on empty. See if the most common reasons for skipping breakfast sound familiar: too rushed in the morning; not hungry at that time of day; or skipping breakfast to try to lose or maintain weight.

If you regularly skip breakfast because it's hard to eat when you're scrambling to get ready for school, take a minute or two the night before to make a breakfast you can enjoy on the run. Or, better yet, go to bed a half-hour earlier so you can buy yourself a few spare minutes in the morning.

If you're in the habit of skipping breakfast because you're not hungry in the morning, you might have to start with a very light breakfast (e.g., half a bagel or a small bowl of cereal) until your body gets used to eating at that time of day. Also, stop to consider what you ate the night before. If you loaded up on a lot of filling snacks after dinner, your body simply might not be ready for food quite yet. The solution is simple: go light on the after-dinner snacks.

And as for the third reason for not eating breakfast, let's take a moment to set the record straight. People who skip breakfast burn 4 to 5 percent fewer calories over the course of the day because their metabolisms slow down to adjust to the "starvation" conditions. Bottom line? Skipping breakfast can actually cause you to gain weight over time.

Chew on This!

Feel hungry enough to eat your pencilcase halfway through the morning? Chances are you didn't have enough **protein** at breakfast. If you have carbohydrates (like a piece of toast) but no protein (like peanut butter) you'll run out of steam sooner. But when you eat them together, your body breaks down sugar more slowly, giving you longer-lasting energy.

Chew on This!

A recent study found that only 67 percent of sixth-grade girls and 47 percent of eighth-grade girls eat **breakfast** on a regular basis.

Smart-Start Smoothie

Here's a simple and delicious way to enjoy breakfast on the run.

Toss the yogurt, fruit, and ice cubes in your blender and process until smooth.

125 mL (1/2 cup) of plain or fruit-flavored yogurt (depending on how sweet you like your smoothie!)

1 banana

125 mL (1/2 cup) of fresh strawberries (or any other fruit you'd like)

250 mL (1 cup) of ice cubes

Pour into a glass and eat with a spoon or sip through a wide straw. Enjoy!

You *Can* Make a Difference!

Imagine how boring the world would be if we all looked exactly the same: if we all had the same color hair and wore the same style of clothing. It would be like being part of a massive chain of paper dolls, identical in every way because no one dared to grab a pair of scissors and break free.

Now that you've read this book, you should have plenty of ideas about what you can do to break free from the chain that says we all have to look the same way.

You can stop and consider how **media messages** affect the way you feel about yourself, and how you judge other people around you.

You can think about the huge **pressures** that girls and women feel, pressure to measure up to an ever-changing definition of what it means to be beautiful.

You can take care of yourself—both **body and soul**.

You can **encourage** other people around you to work with you to create a more body-friendly world.

You can make a difference. All you have to do is dare to be true to yourself

and to celebrate all the things that make you different and special.

MORE BODY TALK

Looking for some additional information on body image, nutrition, and fitness? Grab that mouse and surf on over to these body-friendly web sites.

A Girl's World
www.agirlsworld.com

A chatty site that dishes up the dirt on friends, dating, body image, and other hot topics.

About-Face
www.about-face.org

Combats the negative and distorted images of women that bombard us every day. Their "Gallery of Offenders," highlighting advertisers who go too far, is definitely worth a look.

Dads and Daughters
www.dadsanddaughters.org

A web site that seeks to provide tools "to strengthen father-daughter relationships and to transform the pervasive cultural messages that value daughters more for how they look than for who they are." A great site to check out with your Dad.

GirlSite
www.girlsite.com

A feel-good site that features a gallery of "phenomenal women" who have made a difference in the world. A great place to visit for inspiration!

Girl Power
www.girlpower.gov

The U.S. Department of Health and Human Services' web site for 9- to 14-year-old girls.

Girls Inc.
www.girlsinc.org

A web site that seeks to inspire all girls to be "strong, smart, and bold"—and that serves up a healthy side dish of inspiration at the same time. You'll want to share this site with your sister or your best friend.

Girls Life
www.girlslife.com

The creation of the same team that brought you the magazine of the same name. If you've got questions about your body and how it works, you'll want to check out the site's Body Q&A feature.

GURL
www.gurl.com

A no-nonsense, tell-it-like-it-is guide to anything that's on your mind.

New Moon Publishing
www.newmoon.org

The web site of the highly acclaimed girls' magazine of the same name. Includes details on the "Turn Beauty Inside Out" campaign to promote healthier body image.

SmartGirl
www.smartgirl.com

Provides frank reviews of cosmetic and other products, including some reviews that must make the manufacturers cringe! This is your chance to speak your mind about products that failed to deliver—or to rave about those that have scored big points with you and your friends.

TeensHealth
www.teenshealth.org

Hundreds of articles and Q&A on keeping fit and healthy, body, mind, and soul.

The Way We Look
www.media-awareness.ca

A site that raises awareness of the messages sent by TV, film, video games, newspapers, advertising, and popular music.

Special thanks
to the girls who contributed to this book:

Eliza Pearl Arless
Laura Beck-Andrews
Melissa Brown
Alicia Chamberlain
Sara Clark
Sara Cooper
Laura Crump
Talia Dimerman
Amanda Dossett
Ria Dubois
Jennifer Hanson
Nancy Kovacs
Deirdea Lawrenson

Emma Lewis
Dana Madhill
Leah McEachern
Mary Noah
Leia Pengelly
Katelyn Provo
Brianna Radnor
Helen Redpath
Drew Reynolds
Miranda Thyssen
Kayla Vollrath
Amanda Wedge
Emma Yates

And more thanks
to our technical reviewers:

registered nurse Laura Devine

Sandra Susan Friedman, **author of** *When Girls Feel Fat*

Linda Omichinski, R.D., **President and Founder of HUGS International Inc. and author of** *You Count, Calories Don't*

fitness instructor Jenna Stedman

Carol Weston, **author of** *Girltalk: All the Stuff Your Sister Never Told You*

Index